MY MIND IZ POWERFUL

Kinyin Montaque

John 10 verse 34-37

Let's starts off by building a solid foundation for ourselves. By simply just letting GLOW and Let God.

Glow is actually an acronym that is applicable to the eternal "light" within side of you which makes you the Illuminated one.

G – Gratitude

Being thankful for the things that you do have equates to more of that in abundance.

L – Love

Love Iz Law and precious babies demonstrates that perfectly.

O — Operator

You are the only one that has the joysticks to your Super-Body Intelligence. You could either create or destroy its all up to the operator.

W — Wisdom

Everything starts internal. Such as the word Wombmen which pertains going inward. With the wisdom being applied it makes an individual a WISE 1ne. "W" is also an "M" upside down, which symbolizes the Masculine, being attached to willpower.

These are the core essentials that you have to show yourself.

Are you capable of doing whatever brilliant idea comes to your God mind? HEAVENLY YES!

You have innate superpowers that dwells within your mind and vibrate throughout your entire body. This power is stardust — intelligent atoms or crystalline energy that listens to your every word, taking direction from you and responding to what you are constantly speaking on, bringing it outwards through your powerful God mind into reality.

This power is cosmic dust , which is super intelligence. These atoms are active even when we are resting it's always listening to us on a daily. This cosmic energy has been in us since birth and has never left our side. It can never be taken away — unless we choose to give it away.

You can accomplish absolute anything that comes through your genius mind in which it'll have positive outcomes. Everyone has a different mind set, as well as looks which makes everyone unique in their own way.

Each of your thoughts come across your mental TV screen like clouds. Some can be absurd and most can be in alignment, you just have to decipher through them and choose the one that best suits your Super Shei-Ro/Hei Ro story role. You can take looking up into the starry sky at night and see the comparison of your mind in how vast it is. As it iz in Heaven, so it iz on Earth and you have liberating access to it whenever you so wish. No separation from home base everything is connected.

The most supreme ideas are born from an individual's thoughts and the willpower to believe in themselves, no matter who thinks their ideas are silly or foolish. When you are serious about what you envision in your God mind then it will get to working behind the scenes.

The greatest things that landed on this earth plane came from from one's own mind – and that mind is no different from yours. Everyone is all walking stars, that is operating an intelligent physical machine through your God mind, and that is what gives you right to acknowledge your God mind.

Focus on every detail of the things that you'd like to bring forth in your life experience.

How does it feel in your hand, what color is it, how does it make you feel, your reaction to it. Really see yourself having it in heaven(mind) with lots of emotions tagging along behind it.

Your Dark Infinite Mind is in control of all of your body parts and they're constantly communicating back and forth amongst each other.

You all have the Divine Capacity to do whatever feels right in your heart despite any telephone story that has held you back by one's own mental replay of it.

The mind speaks in encryptions and thats where dreams can be a bit perplexed, simply because that's your triple darkness God mind communicating with you trying to bring something up to your attention. The most powerful thing is that everyone has their own special chip inside of them that is encrypted specifically for their odyssey here on earth..

Preparing your mind for something you know for sure is to come requires a lot of mental repetition(reps). You can strengthen your god mind by Listening to audios, writing them down on paper, or reading some of your favorite books.

Believing in thyself wholeheartedly plays a vital role, because on the inside you can overcome anything once it is seen vividly. Once you acknowledge that this power is there to be utilized, you can transform your life. Your God mind will always work for you to bring your goals into fruition..

Your God mind will bring things, people and situations into your life that will shift you toward the mental pictures you have been displaying, with your emotions attached.

Make sure to always focus on the task that you are working on and also fine tuning it to your liking. The more you absorb your divine ideas and physically work towards them, you will see indicators on the earth plane letting you know you've been heard and things are working for you in the background. Everything you want to accomplish or obtain has always been dwelling inside of you.

You'll then realize that you're an excellent creator!

You are no stranger to the God mind because the same God mind that was being utilized from the genesis, is the same God mind that is placed inside of you from Shei Almighty!

You must also know that before your existence there were elders before you, knowing their connection with the stars and our connection with the earth realm that we live on, through the powers of their God mind, through studying the earth from North to South and from West to East grasping their connections with everything on this earth plane.

Just like the most delicious home cook meal from granny house takes time, so too does your ideas and plans. So having patience with ourselves without comparison can really be to our benefit in the long haul and just gno that our meal is in route!

Talking with close friends or loved ones that share the same amazing mind as you could be very helpful. You could be overthinking, and your close ones could give you energy to keep moving forward and offer lots of encouragement. Getting a different point of view from someone else can also trigger more creative ideas.

We all have the capability to envision whatever we'd like to create around us, forming things with the power of our thoughts, and then conduct the movements in the physical.

Having a blueprint is also essential by really sticking to what one has planned for themselves and never losing sight until it has been reached.

Sending positive thought waves to our God mind is the key to it all and one major way we could send constant re-assurance to our God mind is through I AM affirmations. The coolest thing about affirmations is you can state them just how you would like.

Example: I Am Intelligent!

I am Amazing!   I Am Protected!

I am a Winner!   I Am Safe!

I Am Loved!   I Am Heroic!

I Am Love!   I Am Connected!

I Am The greatest of all times!   I Am EVERYTHING!

You must also remember that your physical body like your fingers, hands and arms acts as workers to put forth the actions that's in your subconscious mind (Deep Mind). Sub as in Submerge or Submarine they all go within the deep regions in our God mind that has great correlations with Shei/Hei ALMIGHTY. We can figure out any confusing situation through listening and communicating with our god mind so that it can communicate back with us through Dreams, Signs and Symbols.

You must go out and do what you've envisioned in your god head to activate it in your physical reality. Working towards something that you really want takes time with a sharp vision. You will get tested with some friction to see how bad you want it, but nothing is impossible & failure only truly occurs whenever we choose to give up or quit on ourselves.

Thinking positive can be a beautiful battle, in which you can defeat any opponent with, and of course there's a remedy that we all can utilize to help minimize those thoughts.

When silly thoughts temporarily cross the mind, simply switch them with something positive, like a favorite meal that you really enjoy or a goal that is getting ready to be in reach. Deep breathing in and out alone slows time down and pushes those crazy thoughts straight of your body.

Negative thinking always passes over by us confronting them with positivity, then new thought bubbles forms over us like a cool sunny day awakening after the storm.

Breathing is also a huge deal because it helps you ponder on what the root of the problem is and where the thought could have originated from because it's not us and it doesn't serve our greater good. No need to swim in the negativity because they will pass over like always just as if it was raining outside followed by the sun rising to bring forth a new day.

You can implement whatever you are wanting into your everyday life so your actions are aligned with your thoughts. Take note everything has a has a flip side to it like a coin, dollar bills, positive and negative thoughts, prince/princess, king/queen and the list goes on. When negative thoughts are temporarily in the way, simply listen and move on to another thought that serves your heart good, as negative and fearful thoughts are harmful thoughts to whisper to yourself when operating your God mind.

Smiling and being in Bliss really boxes negativity out of your sphere. Fearful thoughts or any thoughts that make you feel miserable inside are ones that need to be trashed!

Those thoughts can harden and turn into matter, in which our goals and doing super fly things ONLY matter!

Positivity in all forms is negativity's equal opponent, and whichever one you decide to step into will play out for you.

We cannot lose connection with our imagination powers because we have this God force within us that doesn't have an expiration date. We can mold our God mind just how we'd like and it'll shift things in place for us just how we requested. We are one with all things and we can accomplish whatever we implant into our God mind in assimilation to our divine self , according to the blueprint of our spirit.

Speaking positively not only charges up our inner crystals but it also charges up the inner water that's within side of us. From the water we left to the water we go.

People will then see the end results of the work that has been brought to fruition through our God MIND And the most beautiful thing is we can create and display this as many times as we'd like. Be empowered of what it is that you'd like to do or become, repeat it over and over in your flawless God mind when you wake up, throughout the day and even before you close your eyes for bed at night. This is how we can have full control of our life by never cutting off our imagination line that we all have that's flowing within us.

GLOSSARY:

Assimilation - Being the same or in congruent with another thing.

Assure - State positive things, throwing away any negative thoughts.

Blueprint - A game-plan or map tailored specifically to your mission.

Capable - Someone who has the skill or qualities necessary to do a certain task or can do most things well.

Contrary - Opposite.

Divine - One who is righteous and moves with love.

Ecstatic - Expressing a feeling of joy or happiness.

Embedded - Fixed into the surface of something.

Empowered - Entitled or authority that one has in their own being.

Envision - Displaying clear pictures in your inner mind.

Existence - Having a functional mind and body here on earth.

Fruition - A plan or goal that falls through successfully.

God - The infinite or the all-knowing.

Illuminate - Shiny one being illuminated with wisdom and light energy.

Infinite - Endless or limitless.

Intuitive - Inner voice or inner knowing.

Liberating - Free.

Odyssey - Journey or commute to somewhere.

Operate - Function or work.

Outlandish - Crazy or insane.

Perplex - Confusing or puzzled.

Ponder - To think heavily about something.

Repetition - Repeating something back-to-back in a sequence.

Shei/Hei Almighty - Masculine and feminine being one. Existence and collaborating with each other, just like our left and right brain that need each other to move in rhythm.

Stardust - Star particles and dust, symbolic of the dirt on earth that is in us all.

Supernatural - Something or someone that operates from what is unusual or abnormal.

Transform - Rearranged completely into a better form than the original.

Vividly - Crystal-clear images or visuals seen with the two eyes or in one's mind.

www.ingramcontent.com/pod-product-compliance
Lightning Source LLC
Chambersburg PA
CBHW040916100426
42737CB00042B/95